Do I NEED It? Or Do I WANT It?

Making Budget Choices

Jennifer S. Larson

Lerner Publications Company

Minneapolis

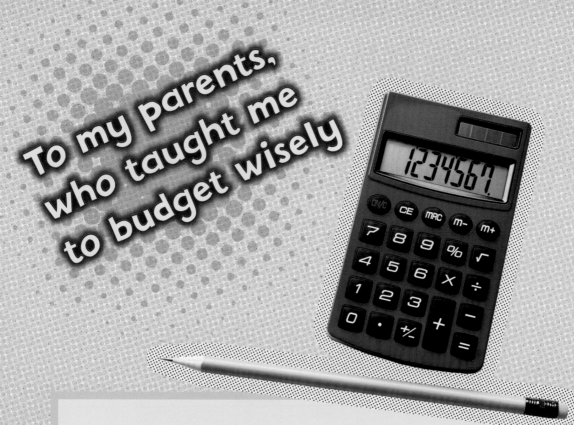

To my parents, who taught me to budget wisely

Copyright © 2010 by Lerner Publishing Group, Inc.

Lerner Publications Company
A division of Lerner Publishing Group, Inc.
241 First Avenue North
Minneapolis, MN 55401 U.S.A.

Website address: www.lernerbooks.com

Library of Congress Cataloging-in-Publication Data

Larson, Jennifer S., 1967–
    Do I need it? Or do I want it? : making budget choices / by Jennifer S. Larson.
        p.   cm. — (Lightning Bolt Books™—Exploring economics)
    Includes index.
    ISBN 978-0-7613-3914-4 (lib. bdg. : alk. paper)
    1. Finance, Personal—Juvenile literature. 2. Budget—Juvenile literature. I. Title.
HG179.L267 2010
    332.024—dc22   2009027459

Manufactured in the United States of America
1 — BP — 12/15/09

Contents

spending Money

Did you ever get money for your birthday? Or maybe a neighbor paid you for raking leaves.

Did you spend your money right away?

How do you decide what to do with your money?

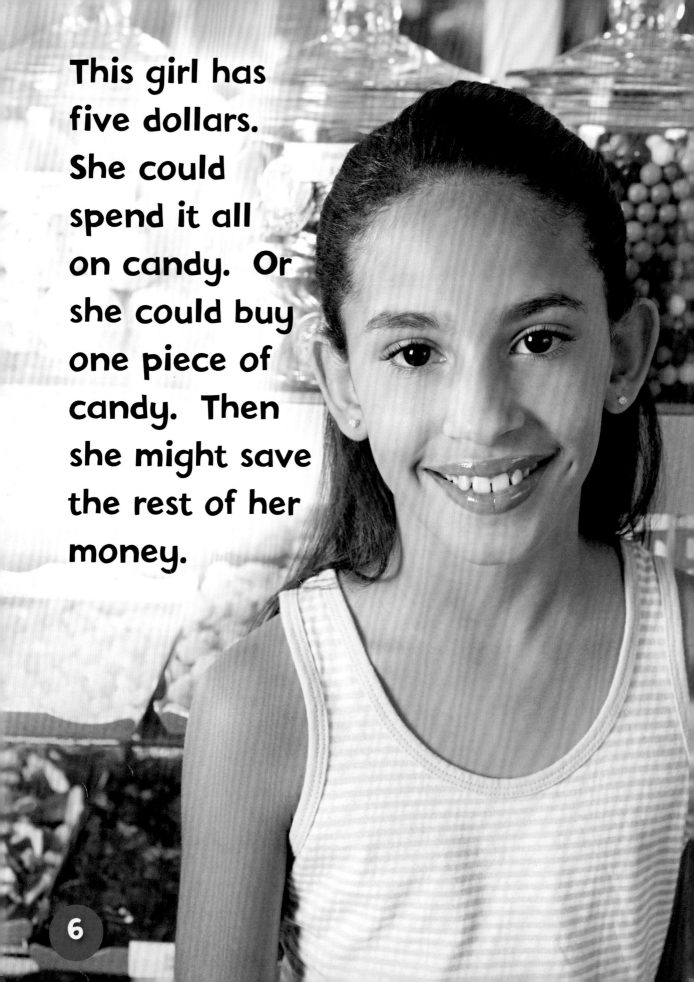

This girl has five dollars. She could spend it all on candy. Or she could buy one piece of candy. Then she might save the rest of her money.

When she saves enough money, she could buy this camera.

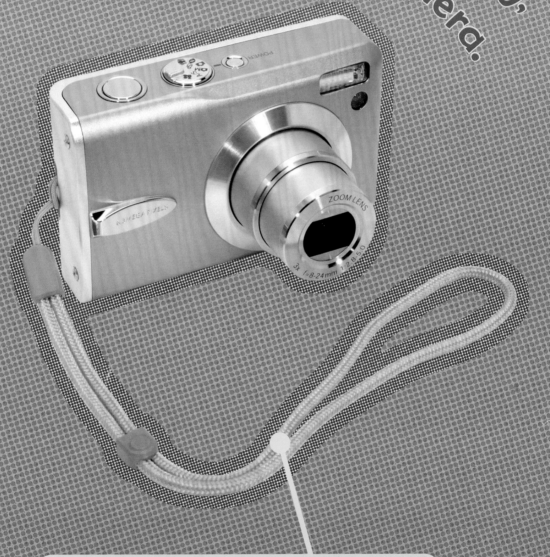

Saving money can help people afford things such as cameras, toys, or video games.

Making Choices

We all need to buy goods and services. Goods are things we can touch. We eat, wear, and use goods.

This girl is picking out marbles at a toy store. Marbles are goods.

A service is something a person does for someone else. A haircut is a service.

What if we don't have enough money to buy all the goods and services we want? We have to choose how to spend our money.

Budgets

We can make a budget to help us decide how to use our money.
A budget is a plan for spending and saving money.

Writing a budget helps us keep track of our money. It helps us plan for the future.

Families make budgets. First, the family needs to know how much money it has. When someone in the family works at a paid job, he or she earns money. This money is called income.

These people are at work earning income.

All the money family members earn is income. To make a budget, a family needs to know how much income they make each month.

This man earns income by building things.

Wants and Needs

Next, a family decides what goods and services it needs that month. Food is a good we need. A place to live is a need. Candy is not a need!

This family is looking at a new house. A home is a need.

A family must first plan to spend money on things it needs.

This woman is looking carefully at her grocery list. Which things from the list does her family need?

This family has money left after buying the things they need. How will they spend their money?

Families talk about how to spend their money.

Many people share their money with other people who need it.

Family members might spend some of their money on things they want. Wants are things we don't need to live. New carpet is a want. A bicycle is a want.

A family might have to choose between the carpet and the bicycle.

A new bicycle is a want. How will this girl's family decide if they should buy one?

How will they decide?

Saving

When families make a budget, they often decide to save some money every month. People save money for things they might need or want later.

This family is planning a vacation. A vacation is a want that people save up for.

Some people save their money in a jar. Other people save money at a bank.

This woman is taking her child to the bank.

21

Banks keep our money for us.

We can get our money back when we need it.

These boys are filling out forms to put their money in the bank.

A family might need money later for an expensive car repair. Or maybe they are saving up for a trampoline!

Do you get an allowance every week? How will you spend your money? Is there something you want to buy now?

This boy is getting an allowance. An allowance is money that is given to someone regularly.

Maybe you are saving for something to buy later. **How will you budget to save for it?**

This girl is creating a budget on a computer.

Who Budgets?

Families are not the only ones who make budgets. Schools, cities, and businesses make budgets too. They have to decide how to spend their money. They have needs and wants, just as families do.

These school board members are talking about their school's budget.

What will
you do
with your
money?

27

Make a Budget

You can make your own budget. First, decide if you want to budget for a day, a week, or a month. Write the dates you'd like to budget for on the top of a sheet of paper.

Next, write down your income. This could include an allowance, money you earned by doing dishes, or money you got as a gift. Add your income together to get a total.

Then, list your expenses. Expenses might be movie tickets, money you gave to help others, or money you put in a savings account. Add your expenses together to get a total.

Finally, subtract your expenses total from your income total. The amount you end up with is how much you have left over to save or spend.

My Budget

Week: Oct. 5 - Oct 12

Income

Allowance: $4.00

Earnings: for cleaning the garage $2.00

Other: gift from Grandpa $3.00

Total: $9.00

Expenses

Savings Account: $4.50

Donation to animal shelter: $1.00

Ticket to fun fair: $.50

Total: $6.00

Income total minus expense total

$9.00
-$6.00
=$3.00

$3.00 left over to save or spend!

Here's a sample budget.

Glossary

allowance: money that adults in some families regularly give to the kids

bank: a business that keeps our money for us

budget: a plan for spending and saving money

earn: to get money for work done

goods: things you can touch that can be bought and sold

income: money a person earns or receives

need: goods and services people must have to live

save: to keep money for later

service: work done by people for others

want: goods and services people do not need to live

Further Reading

Banking Kids Page
http://www.bankingkids.com/pages/elem.html

Einsprunch, Andrew. *What Are Budgets?*
Huntington Beach, CA: Teacher Created Materials,
2008.

Hill, Mary. *Spending and Saving.* New York:
Children's Press, 2005.

It's My Life: Money
http://pbskids.org/itsmylife/money/index.html

Larson, Jennifer S. *What Can You Do with Money?:
Earning, Spending, and Saving.* Minneapolis:
Lerner Publications Company, 2010.

Nelson, Robin. *What Do We Buy?: A Look at Goods
and Services.* Minneapolis: Lerner Publications
Company, 2010.

Index

Photo Acknowledgments

The images in this book are used with the permission of: © iStockphoto.com/filonmar, p. 2; © iStockphoto.com/Rich Legg, p. 4; © Jose Luis Pelaez/Blend Images/CORBIS, p. 5; © Image Source/Getty Images, p. 6; © iStockphoto.com/216 Photo, p. 7; © Todd Strand/ Independent Picture Service, pp. 8, 22, 31; © Julie Caruso, p. 9; © Jutta Klee/CORBIS, p. 10; © Norman Pogson/StockphotoPro.com, p. 11; © iStockphoto.com/Michael DeLeon, p. 12; © iStockphoto.com/ Mark Morgan, p. 13; © Larry Dale Gordon/StockphotoPro. com, p. 14; © Jon Feingersh/Photolibrary, p. 15; © Kevin Cooley/Stone/Getty Images, p. 16; © Purestock/Getty Images, p. 17; © Avava/Dreamstime.com, p. 18; ©Julie Caruso/ Independent Picture Service, pp. 19, 23; © Ed Bock/CORBIS, p. 20; © Geoff A Howard/ Alamy, p. 21; © John Howard/Lifesize/Getty Images, p. 24; © Jurgen Falche/ StockphotoPro.com, p. 25; AP Photo/ Jeff T. Green, p. 26; © Dave & Les Jacobs/ Photoconcepts/CORBIS, p. 27; Reflexstock/BlendRF/Jose Luis Pelaez Inc, p. 30.

Front cover: © iStockphoto.com/Andras Csontos (scooter), © iStockphoto.com/George Pchemyan, (socks).